CATHOLIC † PRIMARY

ETHEROW STREET
LONDON SE22 0JY
TEL 081-693 6852
FAX 081 693 2958

FORWARD IN FAITH

ST. ANTHONYS

Get set... GO!

Squeak and Roar

Sally Hewitt

Photography by Peter Millard

Contents

Watts Books

London • New York • Sydney

Introduction

Listen! The world around you is full of sounds.
Babies cry, traffic hums and grumbles,
machines whirr, dogs bark
and rain patters down.

You can fill your stories,
puppet shows and plays
with sounds too.

Get ready to roar like a lion
and whoosh like the wind.
Make the sound of rumbling thunder
and flapping wings.
Listen to the cauldron bubble
and the fire crackle.

Voice

Get ready

✔Your voice

...Get set

Try making different sounds.
Can you buzz, hum, growl and squeak?
Pop your cheeks.
Click your tongue.
What do you sound like?

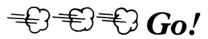 **Go!**

Make a spooky sound like a ghost.
oooooooooOOOOOOOOOooooooooo!
Roar fiercely like a lion.
rrrroooooOOOOAAAARRRR!
Whoosh like the wind.
wwwhhhHHHOOOoooossshhh!

5

Loud hailer

Get ready

✔Thin card   ✔Scissors   ✔Sticky tape

...Get set

Cut out a large circle of card.
Fold it in half and cut along the fold.
Fold one half into a cone shape
and stick its edges together.
Cut an opening in the narrow end
big enough to speak into.

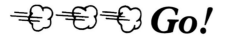 **Go!**

Squeak, howl and roar into the cone.
Your voice will sound louder.
Put a crumpled tissue into the cone.
It will muffle your voice and make it softer.

Footsteps

Get ready

✔ Two plastic pots

✔ Two small wooden blocks

✔ Tray

✔ Sand or salt

...Get set

Sprinkle the sand or salt on to the tray.

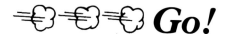 **Go!**

'Walk' the two pots on a table top and in the tray of sand or salt. Do they sound like footsteps? Now try the wooden blocks. Can you make the footsteps run, jump and dance?

Rain and hail

Get ready

- ✔ Rice
- ✔ Dried peas
- ✔ Colander
- ✔ Metal tray

...Get set

Pour some rice into the colander.
Hold the colander over the tray.

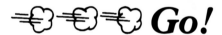 *Go!*

Shake the colander gently
to make the rice fall through the holes
and on to the tray.
Listen.
It sounds like pattering rain.
Drop the peas through your fingers
on to the tray to make the sound of hail.

Flap and rumble

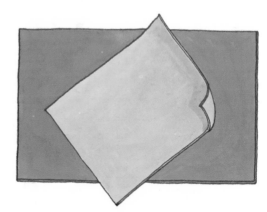

Get ready

✔ Very big sheet of card
✔ Smaller sheet of card

...Get set

Hold one end of the small sheet of card.
Hold both ends of the big sheet with a friend.

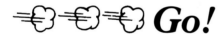 *Go!*

Shake and wobble the big sheet
to make the sound of rumbling thunder.

Flap the smaller sheet
to make the sound of wings.

Bang!

Get ready

✔ Square of card
✔ Glue or sticky tape
✔ Scissors

✔ Square of brown paper
  bigger than the card

...Get set

Cut the brown paper in half
to make a triangle.
Place it diagonally
across the card square.

Fold over the edges and stick them underneath.

Go!

Fold the card in half to make another triangle
with the paper inside.
Hold the corner and flick it downwards.
The paper will shoot out with a loud bang!

Bubble trouble

Get ready

✔ Pots

✔ Bowls

✔ Bottles

✔ Washing up liquid

✔ Water

✔ Long straw

...Get set

Put some water and
a drop of washing up liquid
into each container.

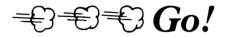 **Go!**

Put the straw in the soapy water and blow.
Each container makes
a different bubbling sound.
You can make underwater sounds
or the sound of a bubbling cauldron.

Splish, splash, splosh!

Get ready

✔ Plastic bottle with a screw top
✔ Water

...Get set

Half fill the bottle with water.
Screw the lid on tightly.

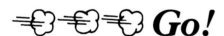 *Go!*

Slop and swash the water around in the bottle.
It sounds like splashing in puddles
or paddling in the sea.
Splish, splash, splosh!

Squeak and scratch

Get ready

✔ Shiny plate   ✔ Cardboard

✔ Sandpaper   ✔ Wooden breadboard

✔ Plastic bottle   ✔ Tin tray

...Get set

Feel the rough and smooth surfaces.

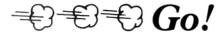 *Go!*

Wet your finger and rub it hard
on the smooth surfaces.
Listen to the different squeaks.
Make a sound like a mouse
and a creaking door.
Scratch your nails lightly on
the rough surfaces.
Make a sound like sawing wood.

Crackle and rustle

Get ready

✔ Tissue paper ✔ Cellophane

✔ Tin foil ✔ Newspaper

...Get set

Crumple the different sorts of paper.
Listen to the sounds they make.

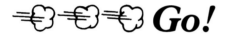 **Go!**

Can you make the crumpled paper
sound like a crackling fire,
a giant munching bones
or leaves rustling in the wind?
What other sounds can you make?

Index

Acknowledgments:
The author and publisher
would like to thank the pupils
of Kenmont Primary School,
London, for their participation
in the photographs of this
book.

©1993 Watts Books

Watts Books
96 Leonard Street
London EC2A 4RH

Franklin Watts Australia
14 Mars Road
Lane Cove
NSW 2066

UK ISBN 0 7496 1437 4

10 9 8 7 6 5 4 3 2 1

Editor: Pippa Pollard
Design: Ruth Levy
Cover design: Mike Davis
Artwork: Ruth Levy

A CIP catalogue record for this
book is available from the
British Library

Dewey Decimal Classification
787

Printed in Malaysia